Virtue

A Short Story of Finding Kindness

Can you search out and find
the ways of kindness both small and great?

Journey with Josianna as she

finds the key of kindness!

Become skilled at

recognizing kindnesses!

Misha Grace Benjamin

Unless otherwise noted, "Vocabulary Definitions at the end of book are quoted from The Merriem-Webster Dictionary and also Vines & Strongs Concise Biblical Dictionary,"

Virtue: A Short Story of Finding Kindness
ISBN-10: 098864035X
ISBN-13: 978-0-9886403-5-1

Virtue: A Short Story of Finding **Kindness**
Published by The Wordflowers Corporation
also known as ®Wordflowers
Copyright© 2013 ®Wordflowers

Library of Congress Control Number: **2013911566**

Your questions, inquiries, and requests for more information are welcome at: info@wordflowerscorp.org. You may also visit our website at www.wordflowers.org. You may also call us at (877)-423-3257 or you may write to us at:

Wordflowers
Post Office Box 406
Occoquan, Virginia 22125

Printed and distributed in the United States of America and Internationally. All rights reserved under International Copyright Law. No part of this book may be reproduced or transmitted in any form or by any means, electronic or mechanical, including photocopying, recording, or by any information storage and retrieval system, without the written permission of the publisher.

"I dedicate this short story to everyone that loves the Lord, wants to do good, and pursue peace."

-Misha Grace Benjamin

Kindness \kĩn(d)-nəs\

Adjective

chrestos(greek): "serviceable, good, pleasant", gracious, kind.

chrestotes(greek): Goodness of heart, gentleness.

philanthropos(greek): humanely, kindly, courteously *(Vines, Page 206).*

Table of Contents

Introduction..1

Chapter 1: Mom's Lost Keys 7
Chapter 1 Review & Study Questions....19

Chapter 2: No Time for Peanut Butter and Banana Sandwiches..........................25
Chapter 2 Review & Study Questions....29

Chapter 3: Josiana's Menacing Attitude and Disrespectful Tone..........................35
Chapter 3 Review & Study Questions....45

Chapter 4: <u>Delightful</u>: Josianna's Day And Mrs. Camador's Dinner Table
<u>Deplorable</u>: Little Brothers......................51

Chapter 4 Review & Study Questions....59

Chapter 5: The Camadora Family Dinner and a Warm Goodnight...........................63

Chapter 5 Review & Study Questions....71

Chapter 6: Josianna's School Day..........77

Chapter 6 Review & Study Questions....91

Chapter 7: The Beginning of a Solitary yet Adventurous Investigation.................97

Chapter 7 Review & Study Questions..103

Chapter 8: Mr. Roger's Ice Cream Parlor 109

Chapter 8 Review & Study Questions..125

Chapter 9:Bakery Keys.........................131

Chapter 9 Review & Study Questions..151

Chapter 10: Mrs. McMatthew's Yard..............................157
Chapter 10 Review & Study Questions...179

Chapter 11: Terrific Baby Brothers.....185
Chapter 11 Review & Study Questions...191

Chapter 12: The Secret Formula of Finding Kindness 197
Chapter 12 Review & Study Questions...203

Vocabulary Definitions................... 204-246

Kindness Key of Conduct Prayer..247

Prayer of Salvation 249

About the Author 251

Other Books Written by the Author 253

For More Information about
Wordflowers 255

References &
Sources...257

Author's Note to the Reader

Dear Readers,

Thank you for choosing to journey with Josianna as she embarks on her own adventurous investigation facing the world to find her Mother's lost keys. In doing so, she finds the key of kindness and learns from her experience to show grace, kindness, respect and love to her family.

Characterizing the moral Christian principal presented by Jesus to love your neighbor as you love yourself this book also gives practice in recognizing and displaying love, service, gentleness, and respect to not only your family but also to your neighbor, who is everyone in the world whom you may have the opportunity to face.

The study & review questions presented at the end of each chapter helps God's children of all ages both young and seasoned to become skilled at seeking the good in diverse situations and recognizing both small and great kindnesses and to appreciate them when they are shown to you. May this book bless your life in Jesus' name! Enjoy!

In the Lord's Kindness,

Misha

Misha G. Benjamin

INTRODUCTION

It is Wednesday, November 2nd, early Autumn season, in Gable, South Carolina and twelve year- old Josianna Camadora is coming home from school after studying with her neighbor and schoolmate Naomi Barkins. Josianna walks across the street to her house. The afternoon sun warms her skin. She pulls her curly dark hair out of her face as she reaches in her school bag to find her house keys. Mistakenly, Josianna forgets to check the mailbox today as her Mother asked her. On this day her Mother was expecting a very important letter. Her Mother, Mrs. Camadora gave her the mailbox keys where her office keys also just happened to be placed on the same key chain.

As she walks up the front steps to her door, Josianna removes her light blue sweater. It is unseasonably warm for the late autumn season. It still feels much like a late summer afternoon. Josianna reaches into her school bag and finds her single house door key attached to a green and brown palm tree key chain. She enters her home and places her school bag on the floor next to a large black coat rack. Her home is warm and welcoming. It smells of her mother's floral perfume still lingering in the air from the early morning hours. Josianna's big and **stately** home is fashioned with dark wooden floors and a huge dark oak banister winding all the way to the top of the stairs leading to the other bedrooms. Her delicate brown hands grasps the banister posts as she walks upstairs to her bedroom to find her 8 year-old little brother Jonah tearing the pages from her favorite novel, *Diary of a young girl*, by Anne Frank.

CHAPTER ONE

MOM'S LOST KEYS

"Don't ever come into my room, you're such a **bothersome** little **terror**! A deplorable little brother!" yells Josianna.

"I'm sorry Josianna, I thought it was o.k." cries Jonah in a small **raspy** voice.

Josianna walks away and stands at the door **furious** at her little brother.

"STAY OUTTA MY ROOM JONAH! AND I MEAN IT! STAY OUT!" she yells firmly pointing downstairs.

Saddened, 8 year-old Jonah, cries as he gets out of her room and runs downstairs to the kitchen.

"YOU COULD'VE ASKED JONAH!" Josianna yells.

Meanwhile, Josianna's Mother, Mrs. Jacquelyn Camadora comes home from her long hours of work from her job as an attorney in Sumter County with the law office of McDaniel, Mathias, and Centron. Mrs. Camadora has worked there for the past ten years after the loss of her husband. Upon arriving inside she finds Jonah in the kitchen reaching for a jar of peanut butter in the pantry. She walks through the kitchen into the living room and checks the tray for her keys which she finds is empty.

"Mom, can you please make me a peanut butter and banana sandwich?" asks Jonah.

"Darling, give me a few minutes, let me get settled and I'll come back down to fix it.

How was your day?" Mrs. Camadora asks Jonah as she makes her way up the winding stairs.

"Mom, I made a paper airplane in my art class and Kahlil made propellers so that it could fly!" says Jonah.

"That's great darling, sounds like you had a good time.

Where is Josi?" asks Mrs. Camadora.

"She's upstairs" says Jonah.

"Josi, I asked you to put my mailbox and office keys back in the tray in the living room after you came home from school. Did you check the mailbox today like I asked you to? Where are the keys?" shouts

Mrs. Camadora as she finally arrives at the top of the stairs with Jonah following closely behind her.

"Jonah took my book out of my shelf without asking and now pages are missing! HE'S SUCH A **BOTHERSOME** LITTLE **TERROR**! A DEPLORABLE LITTLE

BROTHER!" yells Josianna angrily.

"Jonah, what happened?" asks Mrs. Camadora.

"I don't know Mom, I wanted to make an airplane. I couldn't find paper, so...." replies Jonah.

"So, you should've waited until Josi came home and you should have asked her Jonah.

The next time I want you to wait until Josi gets home and then ask her for anything you need Jonah." interrupts Mrs. Camadora.

"Josi, I asked you about the keys. Where are my keys? I need them before Friday." says Mrs. Camadora **sternly**.

Josianna walks back to her room to find her Mom's keys but when she checks her bag, there are no keys there. Mrs. Camadora told her to check the mailbox when she arrived home from school, but she forgot. She looks everywhere in her room and still could not find them.

Chapter One

Study and Review Questions

1. What does it mean to be kind?

_____

_____

_____

_____

_____

2. All **kindness**es must be appreciated and weighed the same. There are none that are too small or too great to show, give, or

share. Can you recognize and find Mrs. Camadora's love, concern, and **kindness** to Josianna and Jonah? Can you recognize and find **kindness** in Josianna and Jonah? Why or Why not?

_____

_____

_____

_____

_____

_____

_____

3. What is Jonah's reaction after Josianna speaks to him in anger? What does he do?

_____

_____

_____

_____

_____

_____

4. What is Mrs. Camadora looking for in the tray in her living room?

_____

_____

5. Does Mrs. Camadora discipline Jonah for tearing the pages out of Josianna's book? What does she tell him? Is this kind/ Is this her job as a Mom? Why? or Why not?

Answers to Study and Review Questions

<u>Possible Answers for Discussion: Chapter One</u>

Consider the following:

1. To be kind means that you are serviceable, good, pleasant, gracious; It also means that you have goodness of heart, and gentleness. Kindness shows that you are humanely, kindly, and courteous to others.

2. <u>Mrs. Camadora</u>: She shows love, concern and kindness to Jonah when she asks him about his day. She says, "How was your day?" (pg. 23) She also asks about Josi? She says, "Where is Josi?" (pg. 24) And she begins to inquire and give attention to her by asking Josianna about a request she had asked of her the day before. "I asked you to put my mailbox and office keys back in the tray in the living room after you came home from school. Did you check the mailbox? Where are the keys? (pg. 24) This can also be viewed as Mrs. Camadora training her daughter in responsibility. Throughout our story we will look closely at how Josianna follows through with her Mother's request.
<u>Josianna</u>: She shows kindness by walking away from her baby brother. Although she is furious, she walks away and stands at her door. She does not hit him or physically abuses him, but she does display verbal abuse by calling him names such as, "a bothersome little brother. A deplorable little terror. (pg. 19-20) Josianna shows serviceable kindness by simply seeking

to find her Mom's keys by checking her bag and looking everywhere in her room. Yet, she still could not find them. (pg. 27-28).

<u>Jonah</u>: He shows gentleness and goodness of heart by sharing with his Mom, his day in art class. He made a paper airplane and His friend Khalil made propellers so it could fly. Jonah also apologizes to Josianna, he says, "I'm sorry Josianna, I thought it was o.k." (pg. 19) Saddened, he cries out of her room and runs downstairs to the kitchen. (pg. 20) Jonah also pleasantly follows closely behind his Mother as she makes her way upstairs (pg. 25).

3. Jonah's reaction after Josianna speaks to him in anger: Jonah apologizes to Josianna, he say's "I'm sorry Josianna, I thought it was o.k." (pg. 19) Saddened, he cries out of her room and runs downstairs to the kitchen. (pg. 20).

4. Mrs. Camadora is looking for her mailbox and office keys in the tray in her living room.

5. Yes, Mrs. Camadora disciplines Jonah for tearing the pages out of Josianna's book. She tells him "So, you should've waited until Josi came home and you should have asked her Jonah. The next time I want you to wait until Josi gets home and then ask her for anything you need Jonah." (pg 26-27). Yes, this is kind and serviceable for a Mom because she is teaching her son Jonah to be respectful and courteous. She is teaching, instructing, and helping Jonah to be kind.

CHAPTER TWO

NO TIME FOR PEANUT BUTTER AND BANANA SANDWICHES

"Oh no!, I lost them." She says softly. *What am I going to do?* she thinks to herself.

Scurrying through her room, Josianna finally sits on the side of her bed trying to figure out what she's going to tell her Mom about her lost keys.

"Mom, I found your notebook and calculator on my shelf! But I believe I left your keys at school. I can walk back now to try to find them if you want?" responds Josianna.

"Josi, it is too late and its' dark outside already. It's 5:30

already! Josi, you are so irresponsible. The school is closed. You need to wait until tomorrow." explains Mrs. Camadora.

"Could you make your brother a peanut butter and banana sandwich?" asks Mrs. Camadora.

"Mom, why do I always have to do things for him? Especially after he tore the pages in my book. I do not have time! I have homework to do!" Josianna shouts angrily.

Chapter Two

Study and Review Questions

1. Is finding her Mom's keys important to Josianna? Why or Why not?

_____

_____

_____

_____

2. Do you understand how Josianna feels about her little brother after he tore the

pages out of her favorite novel? Would you be angry with your little brother too?

_____

_____

_____

_____

_____

3. In this chapter were there any opportunities presented to Josianna to show **kindness** to her little brother? How does she respond?

Answers to Study and Review Questions

<u>Possible Answers for Discussion: Chapter Two</u>

Consider the following:

1. Finding something that was first in your possession and responsibility, such as Josiana's Mother's keys, must be considered important. Josiana shows that finding her Mother's keys is important to her when she scurries through her room attempting and showing effort to look for them. She is quite nervous when she finds they are missing. She finds other things she already has of her mother's in her possession such as her Mother's notebook, and calculator. She also offers to walk back to school to find her Mother's keys.

2. The answers to these questions vary based on each readers own perspective.

3. It is important to take an opportunity to be kind when it is offered or presented. Josianna's Mother offered her the opportunity to prepare a peanut butter and banana sandwich for her baby brother Jonah. She responds by complaining. She feels that she should not have to always do things for him, especially after he ruined her book.

3b. How would you respond? (answers to this question varies because of the individual perspective of each reader.)

CHAPTER THREE

JOSIANNA'S MENACING ATTITUDE AND DISRESPECTFUL TONE

Tired and **exasperated** from a long days work, Mrs. Camadora takes off her high heel shoes and walks into her bedroom. Jonah quickly follows behind her, hugging her waist, and looks up at her.

"Mom, I missed my snack today. Can you show me how to make a peanut butter and banana sandwich?" asks Jonah.

"No honey, Josianna will show you. I have to fix dinner before it gets any later." explains Mrs. Camadora.

"Josi, come here!" calls Mrs. Camadora **strict**ly.

"Let us go down to the kitchen for dinner." says Mrs. Camadora.

The family then makes their way down stairs to the kitchen.

When they enter the kitchen, Jonah reaches the counter for the whole wheat bread.

"Josi can you open the bread for me?" asks Jonah.

"Well, we'll need lots of peanut butter, and a banana." Josianna speaks craftily.

"I'll get the peanut butter!" says Jonah. At an instance, Jonah grabs the peanut butter jar from the pantry and places it on the counter next to Josianna. Josianna opens the peanut butter and scoops out a large tablespoon of nutty peanut butter and begins to spread heaping globs of it onto the whole wheat bread. She then peels open a ripe yellow banana and slices it with a butter knife unto the other side of the peanut butter bread.

"Um, I missed my snack today and I'm hungry Josi." Screeches Jonah.

"Here Jonah, your sandwich is ready." Josianna says

menacingly as she grabs the sandwich from the counter.

As Josianna prepares to hand the sandwich to Jonah, she smudges it into his face.

"Opps!" Josianna shrieks as the sandwich falls from Jonah's face to the floor, smearing peanut butter and banana. Josianna chuckles as she walks out of the kitchen and into the living room making her way upstairs.

"Josi, get back here and apologize RIGHT NOW. Clean up this mess NOW!" yells Mrs. Camadora, **sternly**.

"Mom, I told you, I HAVE HOMEWORK." yells Josianna in a **harsh disrespect**ful tone.

"Josi, why must you be so difficult all the time, it would have only taken you five minutes to spend time with your brother and make him a peanut butter and banana sandwich, then you could go and complete your homework. But since you insisted on being unkind to your brother and **disrespect**ful to me, you don't ever have to worry about fixing or preparing anything for him again." yells Mrs. Camadora.

Chapter Three

Study and Review Questions

1. Is Jonah a kind, **polite** and courteous little brother? Is Josianna kind, **polite** and courteous to Jonah? Why? or Why not?

_____

_____

_____

_____

2. Did Jonah deserve Josianna's **harsh** treatment after he tore pages out of her favorite novel? Why? or Why not?

_____
_____
_____
_____
_____

3. How does Mrs. Camadora discipline Josianna? What does she tell her? Is this kind/Is this her job as a Mom? Why? Why not?

Answers to Study and Review Questions

Possible Answers for Discussion Chapter Three

Consider the following:

1a. Jonah portrays great love and affection towards Mrs. Camadora, his Mom by approaching her with a hug around the waist and asking her if she would prepare for him his favorite sandwich. Towards Josianna, Jonah looks to her for direction and help. He's really a kind hearted little brother who displays kindness and politeness (page 42). It is important to note that most children his age (8 years old) would not ask anyone if they had all ingredients at arm's length. Perhaps he might have thought that he would make a mistake or hurt himself with a knife if he were to make his own sandwich.

1b. Josianna is clearly anything but kind to Jonah as shown on pages 46-47 when she smudges his sandwich in his face. She speaks in a harsh disrespectful tone to her mother as shown on page 48 because she doesn't want to clean up the mess she just made in the kitchen. It is important for the reader to see that this was Josianna's opportunity to show kindness to her baby brother in spite of him tearing the pages out of her favorite novel, but Josianna did not recognize or see her opportunity.

2. Jonah did not deserve the harsh treatment after he tore pages out of Josianna's favorite novel because it is important not to return insult for insult or evil for evil, but to do good to others, show kindness, and treat others humanely that good may come to them.

3. Mrs. Camadora disciplines Josianna by telling her that she doesn't ever have to worry about fixing or preparing anything for Jonah again because she insist on being unkind to her brother Jonah and disrespectful to her Mom (page 49). Yes, this discipline is kind because no parent ever wants to see their children fail or miss the mark without correcting and instructing them to become better. This is very kind and serviceable of Mrs. Camadora because she does not want her children to be uncontrolled, rebellious, and wrecking havoc every where they turn.

CHAPTER FOUR

DELIGHTFUL: *JOSIANNA'S DAY AND MRS. CAMADORA'S DINNER TABLE*
DEPLORABLE: *LITTLE BROTHERS*

Josianna runs upstairs to her room and takes her books out of her school bag. She opens her English Literature book to read her homework assignment on Edgar Allen Poe.

This is so boring. Seventh grade is dreadfully boring!

*Having a **bothersome** little **terror** for a little brother is just as deplorable. Deplorable: Vocabulary Word 5: meaning Lamentable, deserving censure or contempt: Wretched...... I'll just finish my teacher's questions and hopefully I'll get* *them right. Tomorrow I'll turn in my assignments ....and let's see.... today after school I went to Mr. Roger's store with Naomi to buy ice cream... then we went to Susan's mother's job at the bakery to have cake........after we left there we stopped off at Mrs. McMatthew's house to clean the leaves out of her yard... maybe I dropped them out of my pocket and into her yard....and lastly we went to Naomi's house to study. I'll have to retrace my steps tomorrow to figure out where I might of left Mom's keys.*

Back downstairs, as Mrs. Camadora prepares dinner, she

looks at the clock to check the time.

It's 6:15pm, I'll have to put the spaghetti on first and brown the meat while the pasta is cooking. How can I get my daughter to get along better with her brother. How can I teach her responsibility? Maybe I need to teach her respect and manners.

Where did I go wrong? God please help me.

Mrs. Camadora finishes preparing dinner and walks into the dining room to set the table. She takes the white antique Victorian dinnerware out of the Oak china and places the plates and serving bowls at each place setting on the table. She reaches out of the bottom drawer and takes out the silverware. She delicately places a fork, spoon, and butter knife at each place settings.

Lastly, she reaches into the china to find three large glasses. As she walks towards the table, Mrs. Camadora places the glasses on the dining room table. She then goes into the kitchen and returns with milk and pours each glass full.

Chapter Four

Study and Review Questions

1. What subject is Josianna studying for her homework assignment?

_____
_____
_____
_____
_____
_____
_____

2. Do you think that Josianna wants to be more responsible? How?

_____
_____
_____
_____
_____

3. Define deplorable.

4. As we discussed in previous Chapter Study and Review Questions, all **kindness**es must be appreciated and weighed the same. There are none that are too small or too great to show, give, or share. Can you recognize and find Mrs. Camadora's love, concern, and **kindness** to Josianna and Jonah? Why? or Why not?

Answers to Study and Review Questions

<u>Possible Answers for Discussion: Chapter Four</u>

Consider the following:

1. Josianna is studying English Literature specifically the Author Edgar Allen Poe for her homework assignment.

2. Josianna shows that she wants to be more responsible as she is thinking to herself. She begins to retrace her steps from the day before considering to go again to these places to find her mother's lost keys.

3. According to Josianna, Deplorable defined means little brothers; Academically, deplorable is defined as Lamentable, deserving censure or contempt: Wretched.

4. Mrs. Camadora shows her love, concern, and kindness to Josianna and Jonah through her sincere service and commitment as a Mother to her family. Mrs. Camadora serves her family the best and makes their time together extra special by serving their food on special dinnerware and by setting their table. This is extraordinary for just a simple weekday dinner night with family. She also asks God to help her to teach her daughter responsibility.

CHAPTER FIVE

THE CAMADORA FAMILY DINNER AND A WARM GOODNIGHT

"JONAH! JOSI! DINNER IS READY!!!" Mrs. Camadora yells up the stairs as she walks back into the kitchen and drains the slippery pasta out of the hot pot and into a pasta bowl. She then mixes the seasoned brown meat with the savory Italian Marinara sauce.

"Wow! Mom, is all of this for us?" Josianna asks as she sits down at the table.

Jonah sits at his seat and quietly waits for the food to come to the table. Mrs. Camadora enters the room with a bowl of hot spaghetti pasta topped with Italian Meatballs and Marinara Sauce.

For the next hour the Camadora family talk and laugh about their busy day at school and work. After the Camadora family enjoys their dinner, they get ready for bed and prepare for school and work the next day. Mrs. Camadora tucks Jonah into his bed, kisses his forehead and says a prayer with him.

As she cuts off his light, she wishes him a good night and walks into the hall towards Josianna's room.

"Josi, are you getting ready for school tomorrow? Did you

finish your homework?" Mrs. Camadora asks.

"Yes Mom, I did!" Josianna replies.

"Don't forget about my keys tomorrow, I need them for my office on Friday. The next time, please be more responsible Josi." Mrs. Camadora requests.

"Sure Mom, I'll do my best to find them." Josianna replies.

As midnight approaches, the night moon **glisten**s on Josianna's windowsill. The night sounds coming from outside echo throughout the Camadora house on this dark cool autumn night. The Camadora family rests

tranquilly in their warm and **grandiose** home as they all prepare for another busy yet **productive** day.

Chapter Five

Study and Review Questions

1. Can you find any **kindness** showed in this Chapter? How was **kindness** showed and by whom? *hint: How does Mrs. Camadora show that she is a caring Mom?_____

_____

_____

_____

_____

_____

_____

_____

2. What two words describe the Camadora family home on this dark, cool, autumn night?_____

_____

_____

_____

3. As reviewed from the Introduction, what day of the week is it? When does Mrs. Camadora need her mailbox & office keys?_____

_____

_____

_____

_____

_____

_____

4. How can Josianna show her Mom that she can be more responsible?

_____

_____

_____

_____

Answers to Study and Review Questions

<u>Possible Answers for Discussion: Chapter Five</u>

Consider the following:

1. Mrs. Camadora showed great kindness in this Chapter to her children. Her character and actions portray her as a good role model and guide for her children. Mrs. Camadora prepares dinner for her family, prays with them and wishes them both a warm good night.

2. Two words that describe the Camadora family home on this dark, cool, autumn night are: 1. Warm and 2. Grandiose.

3. As reviewed from the Introduction, it is Wednesday, November 2nd. Mrs. Camadora needs her mailbox & office keys by Friday, November 4th.

4. By simply making an attempt to look for her Mother's keys, Josianna has already shown that she can be more responsible. Now, all she has to do is investigate to tangibly find her Mother's lost keys.

CHAPTER SIX

JOSIANNA'S SCHOOL DAY

The next Morning Josianna hurries off to school grabbing her school bag filled with books. She quickly strides into the kitchen to grab her lunch off from the breakfast nook counter. Rushing out of the door, she says goodbye to her Mom and meets Naomi outside as they quickly get on the school bus.

"Bye Mom, I'll see you when you get home tonight!" yells Josianna.

"O.K. honey have a good day!" shouts Mom.

As Josianna arrives at school and enters her first class called English Literature, Josianna prepares to turn in her homework assignment.

"O.K. class, you may now come forward to submit your homework assignments," says Ms. McDaniel, Josianna's English Literature teacher.

Josianna sadly, walks to the front of her class and turns in her homework assignment. Anxious about finding her Mom's lost keys, Josianna finds it hard to focus on her studies.

"Josianna how are you doing today?" asks Ms. McDaniel.

"I have lost my Mother's keys, and I don't know where

they are. She needs them by tomorrow. It was my responsibility, but...I just don't know where they are." Josianna replies sadly.

"Oh! Don't worry Josianna, they will show up sweetheart. Today, you must stay focus and keep your mind centered on your studies, and before you know it you will find what you're looking for. I need you to take your mind off, of those keys and concentrate more on your studies." Ms. McDaniel replies.

"....But my Mom needs them by tomorrow and if I don't have them by then, she'll be very angry with me." explains Josianna.

Let me see how you did on your homework assignment last night. Your interpretation of the poem is accurate and good. You have answered your vocabulary definitions correctly... with the exception of one. Deplorable: Little

Brothers?" Ms. McDaniel replies laughing **smug**ly to herself.

"Oh my! Josianna, this is not the right definition. Is everything okay at home? Maybe you need a little more time to refresh and regroup. Is this because of the keys? You should check your locker and other school bags and ask your classmates, and what I will do for you just for today is, I will prepare your homework assignment for the weekend rather than just for tonight. So, there will be no homework for you tonight Josianna. If things are not better by tomorrow, I will need to speak directly with your Mother.

Seemingly, you are a little more **distracted** today than any other. Please don't worry we will fix this." Ms. McDaniel replies.

Josianna spends the rest of her day **heed**ing Ms. McDaniel's advice. She tries her best to **studious**ly concentrate on her assignments and class interactions. At the end of each class, she asks her teachers if anyone has turned in lost keys.

"Mrs. Moltenmyer, has anyone turned in lost keys to this class today?" asks Josianna.

"No dear, not a soul," replies Mrs. Moltenmyer.

Frustrated and somewhat **dishearten**ed Josianna enters her homeroom where her last class meets for the day. She asked her teacher the same question she had been asking all of them all day.

"Has anyone turned in lost keys today?" she asks **desperate**ly.

"No, Josianna, where did you leave them last?" asks Mrs. Richards **Inquisitive**ly.

"I misplaced them yesterday at some point during the day and now, I can't seem to find them." explains Josianna.

"Why don't you retrace your steps and perhaps you will be successful." replies Mrs. Richards.

Chapter Six

Study and Review Questions

1. How does Josianna feels when she enters her homeroom where her last class meets?

_____

_____

_____

_____

2. What does Mrs. Richards instruct her to do?

3. Is Josianna a good student? What does her teacher say about her homework? Did she make any mistakes?

4. All **kindness**es must be appreciated and weighed the same. There are none that are too small or too great to show, give, or share. Can you recognize and find Josianna's teacher's love, concern, and **kindness** to Josianna? Can you recognize and find **kindness** in Josianna? How? or How not?

Answers to Study and Review Questions

Possible Answers for Discussion: Chapter Six

Consider the following:

1. When Josianna enters her homeroom where her last class meets, she feels frustrated and somewhat disheartened. pp82.

2. Mrs. Richards instructs Josianna to retrace her steps from the day before. In this sense, Mrs. Richards confirms Josianna's original inclination and intention.

3. According to her teachers, Yes, Josianna is a good student because she is accurate and correct in the majority of her homework assignment except in her definition of Deplorable which she defines as little brothers.

4. Yes, Josianna's teacher shows great understanding of Josianna's dilemma; she compromises and accomodates Josianna in her personal situation to help her succeed. Josianna shows kindness and goodness of heart by telling her Mom goodbye as she leaves for school. She courteously asks all of her teachers for help in finding her Mom's lost keys.

CHAPTER SEVEN

THE BEGINNING OF A SOLITARY YET ADVENTUROUS INVESTIGATION

That's right! Mrs. McMatthew's yard is probably where I left them. After racking those leaves they could have gone in the garbage. Josianna thinks to herself.

"Naomi, I will need to go back to Mrs. McMatthew's house to see if I left my Mother's keys there. Will you go with me today to help me look for them in the bags of leaves?" asks Josianna.

"Josianna, I am sorry, but I cannot." replies Naomi. "My Mother said I will need to meet my sister at the airport today. She is coming home from college for Thanksgiving and I will be leaving after school with my Dad."

Well I guess I'll have to look for them alone. Josianna thinks, **sob**bing to herself.

"That's alright Naomi, I will find them. I just have to retrace my steps from yesterday." says Josianna as she braces herself for a **solitary** yet adventurous investigation.

"Where are you starting?" asked Naomi.

"Mrs. McMatthew's yard is probably my best bet." said Josianna.

"We played around so much out there on yesterday. How about Mr. Rogers store Josianna?" asked Naomi.

"I don't know, I will need to check each place we went on yesterday." speaks Josianna.

"And you're at it all alone. Good luck Josianna, I will see

you tomorrow. I hope you're successful." replies Naomi.

Chapter Seven

Review and Study Questions

1. All **kindness**es must be appreciated and weighed the same. There are none that are too small or too great to show, give, or share. Can you recognize and find any **kindness** showed in this Chapter? If so, by whom?

_____

_____

_____

_____

_____

2. Where will Josianna begin to look for her Mom's lost keys? What does Naomi suggest?

_____

_____

_____

_____

_____

3. Why can't Naomi go with her?

4. What does Josianna say that she has to do to find her Mom's lost keys? Would you use the same strategy? Why? or Why not? This is a good strategy. What are other good strategies to finding something that is lost?

Answers to Study and Review Questions

<u>Possible Answers for Discussion: Chapter Seven</u>

Consider the following:

1. Despite the fact that she's unable to go with Josianna on her investigation, Naomi wishes her good luck and success.

2. Josianna decides that Mrs. McMatthews yard is the best place to begin her investigation. Naomi suggests that Josianna begin with Mr. Rogers Store.

3. Naomi cannot go with her because her sister is coming home from college, and she must go to the airport with her dad to pick her up.

4. To find her Mom's lost keys, Josianna says that she must retrace her steps from the day before. Other strategies that could be used to finding something that is lost include:

1. Rallying a search party of 2-5 to help you find what is lost.

2. Going to the source of the keys such as the original owners and paying to replace what is lost.

3. Praying to God that someone will find them and give them to you.

CHAPTER EIGHT

MR. ROGERS ICE CREAM PARLOR

Against her better **judgment**, Josianna decides to take Naomi's advice and go first to Mr. Roger's Ice Cream Parlor. As she enters the Parlor the resounding bells attached to the door clash, clap, and ring nosily against the colorful pink and yellow door. The crowded Ice Cream Parlor seats rows of delicious homemade ice creams; 'HOMEMADE WITH NATURAL INGREDIANTS' reads the sign posting at the counter. People come from far towns just to enjoy Mr. Roger's ice cream.

Today was no different. Old couples and children packed the crowded parlor enjoying ice cream cones in their favorite flavors. The late autumn sun reflecting upon the glass parlor window revealed **beam**s of colorful light into the ice cream parlor. As the kids run and play throughout Mr. Rogers store,

Mr. Rogers comes out from the back of the parlor looking **frustrated** and angry at his ice cream attendant.

The back counter is messy and **disorganized**. There are broken ice cream cones scattered all over the floor. Globs of melted ice cream drip from the scooping spoons that lay on the counter. Stains of dried ice cream cover the freezer where frozen ice cream is stored. Colorful ice cream sprinkles, nuts, raisins, and whipped cream spill **obtrusive**ly from each boxed container onto the floor. Mr. Rogers angrily points his finger in the face of his ice cream attendant.

"Clean up this place or you're fired!!!" replies Mr. Rogers angrily.

Mr. Roger's went back into the back room of the parlor. When he came out his assistant followed him.

"Mr. Rogers, I don't know what happened. I pulled the mixing **lever** and the whole thing just shut off. I checked the wires and still it won't budge." speaks the ice cream attendant.

Turning red in the face Mr. Rogers yells angrily, "Well, We'll just have to use the fresh ice cream already made in the freezer! It's enough of that to serve. Now, take the next customer NOW!" demands Mr. Rogers.

The line Josianna is waiting in now extends to the back of the parlor. Waiting for her turn she reaches her hands into her sweater pocket to check for change.

Maybe I will have enough to buy ice cream today. Maybe someone has turned in lost keys too.

Finally, Josianna reaches the front of the line. The money she finds in her sweater pocket, she scatters over the top of the counter.

"Look kid, are you ready? What kind of ice cream do you want?" asks the ice cream attendant. Then suddenly, Mr. Rogers enters the room.

"Mr. Rogers, I was here yesterday, my name is Josianna Camadora. My friend Naomi and I came here after school yesterday and...." explains Josianna.

"Look kid, I don't have all day! Do you want ice cream or not?" interrupts Mr. Rogers.

Looking down at the coins on the counter, Josianna begins to count her money.

Fifty, Seventy-Five, eighty five, eighty six, eighty-seven, eighty-eight cents. "Well, what I wanted to ask you Mr. Rogers, Sir, is has anyone turned in lost keys today?" asks Josianna.

"I don't sell keys! This is an ice cream parlor! If you don't have enough for ice cream get out of my line, you're holding things up kid!" replies Mr. Rogers angrily.

"What!" says Josianna with tears in her eyes.

"I waited this long and you cannot even check to see if someone has turned them in?" asks Josianna.

As Josianna began to cry her soft brown hands gently wipe her tears from her face. She brushes her curls back with the back of her hand as she reaches down to pick up her school bag. Her brown and blue sweater warms her arms and shoulders as she exit's Mr. Roger's store to walk one block to Susan's

mother's job at the bakery.

Chapter Eight

Study & Review Questions

1. All **kindness**es must be appreciated and weighed the same. There are none that are too small or too great to show, give, or share. Can you recognize and find **kindness** in Josianna? How about Mr. Rogers? Why? or Why not?

_____

_____

_____

_____

_____

2. Describe the condition of the ice cream parlor? Is this the best way your ice cream

parlor should be presented to serve your customers?

___

___

___

___

3. Mr. Rogers attitude is seemingly very angry and **disrespect**ful to his ice cream attendant and to Josianna. Is this the best way for an ice cream store manager to speak to his worker and also to his customer? Why? or why not?

___

___

___

___

4. If you were the owner of your own ice cream parlor, how would you have managed the busy ice cream parlor and your attendant as well as Josianna?

5. Can you understand Mr. Roger's frustration, or is there a better way of **kindness** to keep the ice cream parlor running smoothly? How?

Answers to Study and Review Questions

Possible Answers for Discussion: Chapter Eight

Consider the following:

1. Josianna is pleasant, well mannered and polite to Mr. Rogers despite his angry attitude. Obviously Mr. Rogers is a very angry man and he is not having a good day. Despite the fact that others are serviceable, pleasant, polite, and well mannered towards Mr. Rogers, he is still angry.

Despite the busy and disorganized ice cream parlor, Mr. Roger's colorful parlor door and sign reading HOMEMADE WITH NATURAL INGREDIANTS, the lighting in the parlor as well as the reflecting sun all made wanting ice cream inviting. Mr. Rogers does not show kindness because he does not bother to check for Josianna's keys and he speaks very angrily towards her and his workers.

2. The back counter is messy and disorganized. Broken ice cream cones are scattered on the black and white colored square floor. Globs of melted ice cream drip from the scooping spoons that lay on the counter. Stains of dried ice cream cover the freezer where frozen ice cream is stored. Colorful ice cream sprinkles, nuts, raisins, and whipped cream spill obtrusively from each boxed container onto the floor. pp102.

Of course this is not the best way to present your ice cream parlor and serve your customers. Consider maintaining composure under pressure such as a busy ice cream parlor. Although Mr. Rogers found it very difficult to maintain a pleasant attitude and demeanor, do you believe that you can still be pleasant and kind, even when everything around you seem to be array, busy, and falling apart? Most people will find this difficult. Could Mr. Roger's attitude also be his way of keeping things together? Is this the right approach? What about you?

3. No this is not the best way for an ice cream store manager to speak to his worker and also to his customer because as a Manager he must lead by example. Perhaps Mr. Rogers is just having a bad day, perhaps his ice cream parlor is not always in this condition, but he must maintain his composure and try to remain pleasant, kind, courteous, and respectful to both his worker and his customer if he wants anyone to work for him and if he wants anyone to buy his ice cream, he should try his best to be kind, humanely, and serviceable.

4. Answers vary based on individual perspectives.

5. Answers vary based on individual perspectives.

CHAPTER NINE

BAKERY KEYS

The afternoon autumn breeze comforts Josianna as she wipes the tears away from her eyes. She squints her round dark brown eyes as she looks forward counting the blocks ahead until she reaches Susan's Mother's job at the Bakery. *One, Two,....Four, Five...* She counts to herself, holding and pulling the sleeve of her sweater tightly in her hand.

As she passes an antique store in downtown Sumter she looks to the left and gazes into a cloudy, dull window to see a river stream of tear drops pouring from her eyes. *Maybe I left them inside the bakery.* She **sob**s to herself as she wipes her tears with the sleeve of her brown and blue sweater tightly closed in her fist. *It'll be dark soon, I'd better hurry before it gets any later.* Josianna hurries along walking **swift**ly to the seventh block where she sees the pink and red signs reading BAKERY on the front door.

As she walks inside the Bakery, pink walls **inscribe** beautiful flowers in an array of colors. The high ceiling holds a large **chandelier** and other antique lights that brighten every baker's work station.

Each work station is sectioned off by antique Oriental wall dividers designed with flowers. Each baker works intently on cakes, pies, pastries, and other delicious desserts. The musical sounds and smell of cake fills the air and draws Josianna closer to the front of the bakery. Josianna walks quietly to the front and asks the cashier to see Mrs. Nickolson, her friend Susan's mother.

"What a lovely sweater you're wearing today. Give me just a second please. Patty! There is a little lady here to see you. Sweetie, what's your name?" asks the bakery cashier.

"My name is Josianna Camadora maam'." replies Josianna.

"What is wrong dear, you're looking a little blue," says the bakery cashier.

"I lost my Mother's keys and I have looked everywhere and I don't know where they are or how to find them." speaks Josianna.

"Well, let me fix you a slice of apple pie Josianna. It will only take a minute. Have yourself a seat right here and I'll be right back with your pie! How about some milk with that sweetheart?" asks the bakery cashier.

"Sure Maam! That sounds great!" Josianna says, with a smile.

Josianna watches from the front of the Bakery store as Mrs. Nicolson works from her bakery work station. Mrs. Nicolson's pink bakery hat **glum**ly rests flatly on her head. Her strawberry blonde hair is tied in a ponytail and pulled back away from her face.

Her work station is **clutter**ed with large blue and white flour and sugar canisters. A large yellow pitcher filled with milk is placed on her workstation counter also, she grabs a large mixing spoon and measuring cup and fills her bowl with flour, sugar, salt, and baking powder. As she begins to mix her ingredients, Josianna begins to walk towards her. *Her face is filled with red and brown freckles just like Susan. That has to be her Mom, Yes, I remember from yesterday, she has freckles just like Susan.*

Josianna says to herself as she smiles to greet Mrs. Nickolson.

"Hello, Mrs. Nickolson, I am your daughter Susan's friend from school. My name is Josianna and I was here yesterday with your daughter after school. I believe I **accidentally** left my Mother's keys here." Josianna replies.

"Oh! Yes dear, I do recall you from yesterday. What did you say that you needed? I'm quite busy here, as you can see." replies Mrs. Nickolson.

"Keys! Yes, can you please check to see if they were left here or if anyone could have turned them in today?" Josianna asks **polite**ly.

Mrs. Nicholson, complains and shakes her head from left to right, she haughtily puts her hands on her hips and says,

"Honey, that is a shame that you cannot even keep up with something that belongs to your Mother? Of all things precious, whatever is hers should be more precious than anything. Where is your sense of responsibility? There are NO KEYS HERE and I'm not looking for them. You should know better. You and Susan are the same age and I teach her to be responsible. Your Mother needs to do the same with you." Shocked at Mrs. Nicolson's response Josianna swings her arms to the side and clumsily hits Mrs. Nickolson's cake batter bowl. The bowl **accidentally** falls from Mrs. Nickolson's work station and splatters cake batter **brazen**ly all over the Bakery floor and **obtrusive**ly in Mrs. Nickolson's face and hair. Josianna, screams and jumps back yelling, " Oh my gosh,

You're so mean! I just asked if you could help me. I didn't mean to drop your bowl!" Screams Josianna.

"YOU **CLUMSY** LITTLE **BOTHERSOME TERROR!** CLEAN THIS UP RIGHT NOW!!!! OR ELSE I'LL CALL THE COPS." Mrs. Nickolson, yells sharply and angrily.

Josianna tries to run as fast as she can out of the Bakery. As she **swift**s her way out her brown loafer shoes slip off of her feet and she slides and glides on the messy cake batter. As she begins to **momentarily** lose her balance, she grabs a hold of the front door and quickly regains her posture.

Frowning, she quickly opens the front bakery door and walks out slamming the door as hard as she can behind her. "I'm getting outta here now!" Josianna yells.

Chapter Nine

Study & Review Questions

1. All **kindness**es must be appreciated and weighed the same. There are none that are too small or too great to show, give, or share. Who is the one person who shows Josianna **kindness** in the Bakery? How does this person show **kindness** to Josianna? Did anyone else show **kindness** in the Bakery?

_____

_____

_____

_____

_____

_____

_____

2. Does Josianna show **kindness** to anyone in the bakery? Is there **kindness** shown to her? How is **kindness** shown to her? How does she show **kindness**?

_____

_____

_____

_____

_____

_____

3. What condition is the bakery in when Josianna arrives? Describe. What is the condition of the bakery when she leaves? Describe. Was it kind of Josianna to leave the bakery in this condition? What would you have done if you were in her situation?

_____

_____

_____

_____

Answers to Study and Review Questions

<u>Possible Answers for Discussion: Chapter Nine</u>

Consider the following:

1. The bakery cashier shows Josianna great kindness by her good words that contributed positively to the situation, the Bakery Cashier also showed great kindness by acknowledging Josianna as soon as she arrived inside the bakery; she also offered to serve her a slice of apple pie and milk. Josianna shows kindness by asking Mrs. Nickolson very pleasantly and politely if she can look for her Mom's keys.

2. Josianna shows kindness by being good, pleasant and polite to everyone she meets; Only after Mrs. Nickolson conveys that she needs to be more responsible does Josianna become offended and accidentally knocks over the cake batter bowl.

3. <u>Condition of the Bakery as Josianna arrives:</u> As she walks inside the Bakery, pink walls inscribe beautiful flowers in an array of colors. The high ceiling holds a large chandelier and other antique lights that brighten every baker's work station. Each work station is sectioned off by antique Oriental wall dividers designed with flowers. Each baker works intently on cakes, pies, pastries, and other delicious desserts. The musical sounds and smell of cake fills the air and draws Josianna closer to the front of the bakery.

Condition of the Bakery as Josianna leaves: Josianna swings her arms to the side and clumsily hits Mrs. Nickolson's cake batter bowl. The bowl accidentally falls from Mrs. Nickolson's work station and splatters cake batter brazenly all over the Bakery floor and obtrusively in Mrs. Nickolson's face and hair.

If you were in Josianna's situation one alternative you would have would be to just leave as she did because this lady Mrs. Nickolson was threatening to call the cops on her.

If you chose to stay and clean up the accidental cake batter mess you would still be in the right because Jesus says if your enemy hurts you (as Mrs. Nickolson spoke severely harsh to Josianna), you should bless them and turn the other cheek. In this sense, Josianna would have showed great humility, bravery, and boldness; and her behavior would have been pleasing to God because her suffering was undeserved. (1 Peter 2:20 KJV)

CHAPTER TEN

MRS. MCMATTHEW'S YARD

Josianna hurries out of the **chaotic** bakery and walks **circumspect**ly back home taking special care of her surroundings. *I hope Susan's Mother doesn't get me in any kind of trouble.* She looks down at her watch and finds that it is 5:15 p.m. *Well, I guess my Mom will have to order new keys for the mailbox and also for her office. Oh God, please don't let my Mom be angry because I lost her keys.*

Josianna finally arrives one block away from her house. As she passes her next door neighbor, Mrs. McMatthew's yard, she overhears Mrs. McMatthews and her husband arguing.

    Josianna see's Mr. McMatthews pointing his finger angrily at his wife as she looks through the window lattice. His face is frowned and angry. His black glasses hold firmly and closely on his nose. Suddenly, he throws his hands **frenetically** in the air.

"Get outta here you old hag!" shouts Mr. McMatthews.

"No, You get out, this is my house!" yells Mrs. McMatthews.

"You ran up my credit cards spending money on your **elaborate** parties and pinochle group. I wouldn't be surprised if I'd be bankrupt in a matter of weeks the way you are spending." replies Mr. McMatthews.

"Well Harry, if you would have taken the job at the

Laundromat you'd have money for yourself." says Mrs. McMatthews **sarcastically**.

"I've worked 40 years in the Military for this! Delores McMatthews you ought to be ashamed of yourself. Shame on you! You should learn how to treat me the way you would like to be treated. Mark my word!

You will reap what you **sow** Delores McMatthews." says Mr. McMatthews.

    Mr. McMatthews begins to **sob** and shake his head from left to right. **Sob**bing, he sits on a chair, removes his glasses and places both of his hands on his face. Suddenly he looks up to the ceiling, closes his eyes and says a prayer.

"I want a divorce Harry! You are just an old cheap man..." yells Mrs. McMatthews, **sternly**.

"I'd give you a divorce if I didn't love you so much Delores. I don't deserve your **indecent**, mean, and harmful words and attitude," shouts Mr. McMatthews.

Mrs. McMatthews walks into the kitchen and **fumble**s around with pots and pans. She takes leftover food out of the refrigerator and puts it into the oven. She sighs, and goes back into the living room where her husband is sitting.

"Harry, there's food that will be ready soon." says Mrs. McMatthews.

"I guess we shouldn't argue." Mr. McMatthews replies.

"Please forgive me Delores, you're right. I'll take the job at the Laundromat." replies Mr. McMatthews, **repentantly**.

"Delores, I remember you and your **kindness** in our youth, when you treated me with **kindness**. Since I have showed you **kindness**, I just hoped that you will also show **kindness** to me. Let's go back to those times." Mr. McMatthews replies **tender**ly.

Mr. McMatthews puts on his sweater and grabs his walking cane. He comes out on the porch and sits in the rocking chair on the porch as Josianna makes her way back to her home next door. Overhearing the sadness in Mr. McMatthew's voice Josianna begins to think about the way she treated Jonah.

*I suppose it is rather important to treat others the way you would like to be treated. Oh God, maybe that's why everyone was so unkind to me today. I need to tell my baby brother that I love him and that I didn't mean to treat him like a deplorable **bothersome** little terror. I need to apologize to*

*Jonah. Mr. McMatthews is right, you reap what you **sow**. It's far better to treat others the way you would like to be treated. I didn't mean to make him sad and cry. Oh God, I should not have yelled at him and treated him so mean, he's only 8 years old, and I know he didn't tear the pages out of my* *favorite book on purpose. It wasn't even really a big deal; it's just a book that can be replaced. I pray that he will forgive me.*

    Josianna opens the front gate of the entry way to her home. She walks up the front porch steps and grabs her single door key out of her bag of books. As she enters her home she finds her Mom reading in the sitting room near the kitchen. Josianna hangs her bag of books on the coat rack, removes her jacket and hangs it on a hook.

"I didn't find your keys today Mother. I don't want you to be angry with me; I want to show you that I am responsible. Can you please forgive me? I don't know what to do. I didn't find your keys today." cries Josianna, frustratingly.

"It's okay Josianna, **calm** down, I gave you those keys because I know you are responsible and you're becoming a young lady and not just an ordinary teenager. I have **confidence** in you. By the way, you never lost them sweetheart. When you put your school bag and jacket on the coat rack, the keys must have fallen behind the coat rack. Your nanny, Mrs. Consenta found them while dusting today." said Mrs. Camadora.

Relieved, Josianna took a deep breath and sighed.

"I thought I lost your keys, but I finally found someone who has something kind to say to me. Thanks Mom. Everywhere I went today, everyone was quite sour and uncaring." Josianna replies.

"Oh Dear, you must have been terribly **frustrated** looking for those keys and making them the only object in your view." laughs Mrs. Camadora.

"Mom, I think I'm going to apologize to Jonah. I didn't mean to make him sad and cry. I should not have yelled at him or treated him so mean. I would never want anyone to treat me

that way."

Chapter Ten

Study & Review Questions

1. All **kindness**es must be appreciated and weighed the same. There are none that are too small or too great to show, give, or share. How does Mrs. Camadora, Josianna's Mother, show her **kindness** after she arrives home? Were there any other **kindness**es shown in this chapter? If so, by whom?

_____

_____

_____

2. What does Josianna learn from overhearing her neighbors, the McMatthews?

3. Josianna says that no one showed her **kindness** while she was on her investigation to find her Mom's lost keys. Do you believe this is true? Why? Why not?

_____

_____

_____

_____

Answers to Study and Review Questions

Possible Answers for Discussion: Chapter Ten

Consider the following:

1. Mrs. Camadora, Josianna's Mother, shows Josianna great kindness after she arrives home by telling her these words which made the circumstance better: "its o.k. Josianna, calm down, I gave you those keys because I know you are responsible and you're becoming a young lady and not just an ordinary teenager. I have confidence in you. By the way, you never lost them sweetheart. When you put your school bag and jacket on the coat rack, the keys must have fallen behind the coat rack. Your nanny, Mrs. Consenta found them while dusting today."

Mrs. McMatthews also showed her husband kindness by offering to serve him food.

2. Josianna learns from overhearing her neighbors the McMatthews argue that she must apologize to her baby brother Jonah and treat him the way she would like to be treated. Josianna thinks to herself: "Mr. <u>McMatthews is right, you reap what you sow. It's far better to treat others the way you would like to be treated. I didn't mean to make him sad and cry. Oh God, I should not have yelled at him and treated him so mean, he's only 8 years old, and I know he didn't tear the pages out of my favorite book on purpose. It wasn't even really a big deal;</u>

it's just a book that can be replaced. I pray that he will forgive me."

3. It is not true that no one showed Josianna kindness while she was on her investigation to find her Mom's lost keys. As discussed from previous chapters that we've had the opportunity to look at closely, Kindness was found in its smallest form from little Jonah who sincerely apologized to Josianna for tearing the pages out of her book to the bakery attendant at Susan's Mother's job who greeted her upon her arrival and offered to serve her apple pie and milk.

Perhaps Josianna was so consumed on her quest to find her Mom's lost keys that she did not recognize anything good or kind that was shown or done to her. Understandably, her experience frustrated her and as shown from each chapter she had a very wearisome and tiresome day.

CHAPTER ELEVEN

TERRIFIC: BABY BROTHERS

Josianna walks into the kitchen to find Jonah sitting at the breakfast table doing his homework.

"Jonah, are you practicing your spelling words? How are you doing? Do you need some help with your homework?" Josianna asks.

"I can spell all ten of my spelling words on my own Josi!" replies Jonah.

"That's great Jonah! But I have a very special vocabulary word that is not on your list. Can you try to spell my special vocabulary word for you?" Josianna asks.

"Yeah! sure Josi, what is it?" responds Jonah.

"Okay, can you spell the word Terrific?" Josianna asks.

"T-E-R-R-I-F-I-C ?" spells Jonah questionably. "Is that right Josi?" asks Jonah.

"No, that's wrong Jonah. It's J-O-N-A-H, it's you Jonah! I just need you to know that you are my Terrific little brother." Josianna replies.

After careful **consideration** Josianna decides to do something special for her little brother whom she showed anger towards prior. Josianna decides to show him that she really didn't mean any of the angry words she spoke to him.

"Jonah, next week after school, I'll ask Mrs. Consenta to take us to Mr. Rogers Ice Cream Parlor to buy Ice Cream and I'll make everything up to you. Jonah, I Love you. I meant to say you're a terrific little brother and not a deplorable **bothersome** little **terror**! And you tore out all the pages in my book that I didn't need. How did you know?" Josianna asks.

"It's okay Josi, I won't do it again. I love you too Josi!" smiles Jonah.

Chapter Eleven

Study & Review Questions

1. All **kindness**es must be appreciated and weighed the same. There are none that are too small or too great to show, give, or share. How does Josianna attempt to make amends with her baby brother Jonah? Is she successful? Why? or Why not?

_____

_____

_____

_____

2. Define and spell the word Terrific?

3. Throughout this short story, how would you describe Jonah's attitude towards his older sister, Josianna? Is he still kind to her even after she reacted menacing and **disrespect**ful to him? Was this bravery shown anywhere else within this story? If so, by whom?

_____
_____
_____
_____
_____

Answers to Study and Review Questions

<u>Possible Answers for Discussion: Chapter Eleven</u>

Consider the following:

1. Josianna attempts to make amends with her baby brother Jonah by helping him with his homework. She instructs him to spell TERRIFIC and she makes sure that he knows that he is a terrific baby brother. She is successful because he accepts her apology and tells her he won't do it again and that he loves her.

2. Terrific: JONAH and little brothers.

3. Throughout this story Jonah was a strong, brave soul who held his composure when treated unjustly by Josianna. In every circumstance he never retaliated or showed revenge; He even forgives her and receives her back in love. In comparison, Josianna also shows this same bravery when she decides to return to Mr. Roger's store with Jonah and her nanny Ms. Consenta, even after he spoke to her unjustly and mean spirited.

CHAPTER TWELVE

THE SECRET FORMULA OF FINDING **KINDNESS**

"Mom, thanks for understanding! I'm so glad that the keys were finally found. Your lost keys opened the door to helping me show **kindness** to my brother.

The most important key that I have found today is the key of **kindness**: to do onto others what I would have them to do unto me and to treat others the way I would like to be treated. I believe that I can be kind. Sometimes it's hard. But I'll just keep trying and trying until I get it right!" Josianna replies.

"I am so glad Josi that you realize how important it is to show **kindness** to your family. God, I thank you for answering my prayer!" shouts Mrs. Camadora.

"Everywhere I went people were so mean to me and downright rude, until I went to my last stop at Mrs.

McMatthew's house. I learned from the McMatthews that if we all are good and kind to one another there will be peace." responds Josianna.

"Now, when you go out to face the world, you know that you can show **kindness** to all people. Because of God's grace you will receive **kindness** from others and from God because you have showed love and **kindness**. Especially to those closest to you, your neighbor, friends and family. We love you Josi and we will all keep trying to show **kindness** until we get it right." Mrs. Camadora smiles.

THE END.

Chapter Twelve

Study & Review Questions

1. All **kindness**es must be appreciated and weighed the same. There are none that are too small or too great to show, give, or share. What did Josianna realize was the most important key to finding **kindness**?

_____

_____

_____

_____

2. Before you face the world everyday, who helps you to show **kindness** to your neighbor (everyone you have the opportunity to face everyday) according to Mrs. Camadora?

3. What did Mrs. Camadora's lost keys open the door to helping Josianna do?

Answers to Study and Review Questions

<u>Possible Answers for Discussion: Chapter Twelve</u>

Consider the following:

1. Josianna realized that the most important key to finding kindness is treating others the way you would like to be treated.

2. According to Mrs. Camadora, showing kindness to your friends and family helps you to show kindness to your neighbor (everyone you have the opportunity to face every day).

3. Mrs. Camadora's lost keys opened the door to helping Josianna show kindness to her baby brother Jonah.

VOCABULARY DEFINITIONS

ac·ci·den·tally

adjective
1. happening by chance or <u>accident</u>; not planned; unexpected: *an accidental meeting*.
2. nonessential; incidental; subsidiary: *accidental benefits*.
3. *Music.* relating to or indicating sharps, flats, or naturals.
noun
4. a nonessential or subsidiary circumstance, characteristic, or feature.
5. *Music.* a sign placed before a note indicating a chromatic alteration of its pitch.

beam

noun
1. any of various relatively long pieces of metal, wood, stone, etc., manufactured or shaped especially for use as <u>rigid</u> members or parts of structures or machines.
2. *Building Trades.* a horizontal bearing member, as a joist or lintel.

3. *Engineering* . a rigid member or structure supported at each end, subject to bending stresses from a direction perpendicular to its length.
4. *Nautical* .
a. a horizontal structural member, usually transverse, for supporting the decks and flats of a vessel.
b. the extreme width of a vessel.
c. the shank of an anchor.
5. *Aeronautics* . The direction perpendicular to the plane of symmetry of an aircraft and outward from the side.

both·er·some
adjective \ˈbä-<u>th</u>ər-səm\vexing.
: causing bother : VEXING

bra·zen

adjective
1. shameless or impudent: **brazen** *presumption.*
2. made of brass.
3. like brass, as in <u>sound</u>, color, or strength.
verb (used with object)
4. to make **brazen** or bold.
Verb phrases
5. **brazen outthrough,** to face boldly or shamelessly: *He prefers to* **brazen** *it out rather than admit defeat.*

Origin:
before 1000; Middle English *brasen* (adj.), Old English *bræsen* of brass

Related forms
bra·zen·ly, *adverb*
bra·zen·ness, *noun*
out·bra·zen, *verb (used with object)*
un·bra·zen, *adjective*
un·bra·zen·ly, *adverb*
un·bra·zen·ness, *noun*
Synonyms
1, 3. brassy. **1.** insolent, defiant. See bold.

calm

adjective
1. without rough motion; still or nearly still: *a **calm** sea.*
2. not windy or stormy: *a **calm** day.*
3. free from excitement or passion; **tranquil**: *a **calm** face; a **calm** manner.*
noun
4. freedom from motion or disturbance; stillness.
5. *Meteorology*. wind speed of less than 1 mile per hour (0.447 m/sec).
6. freedom from agitation, excitement, or passion; **tranquil**lity; serenity: *She faced the possibility of death with complete **calm**.*
verb (used with object)

7. to make **calm**: *He calmed the excited dog.*
verb (used without object)
8. to become **calm** (usually followed by *down*).

Origin:
1350–1400; (noun, adj.) Middle English *calm(e)* < Italian *calma* (noun), *calmo* (adj.) < Late Latin *cauma* summer heat (with *l* perhaps from Latin *calēre* to be hot) < Greek *kaûma* (stem *kaumat-*) burning heat; akin to *kaíein* to burn (see caustic); (v.) Middle English *calmen* < Italian *calmare,* derivative of the noun

Related forms
calm·ing·ly, *adverb*
calm·ly, *adverb*
calm·ness, *noun*
qua·si-calm, *adjective*
qua·si-calm·ly, *adverb*
un·calm, *adjective* **un·calm·ly,** *adverb*
un·calm·ness, *noun*
Synonyms
1. quiet, motionless. **3.** placid, peaceful, serene, self-possessed. CALM, COLLECTED, COMPOSED, COOL imply the absence of agitation. CALM implies an unruffled state, especially under disturbing conditions: *calm in a crisis.* COLLECTED implies complete inner command of oneself, usually as the result of an effort: *He remained collected in spite of the excitement.* One

who is COMPOSED has or has gained dignified self-possession: *pale but composed*. COOL implies clarity of **judgment** along with apparent absence of strong feeling or excitement, especially in circumstances of danger or strain: *so cool that he seemed* ***calm*. 7.** still, quiet, **tranquil**ize; allay, assuage, mollify, soothe, soften.

Antonyms
2. tempestuous. **3.** agitated.

cha·ot·ic

adjective
completely confused or disordered: *a **chaotic** mass of books and papers.*

Origin:
1705–15; chao(s) + -tic

Related forms
cha·ot·i·cal·ly, *adverb*
non·cha·ot·ic, *adjective*
non·cha·ot·i·cal·ly, *adverb*
sem·i·cha·ot·ic, *adjective*
sem·i·cha·ot·i·cal·ly, *adverb*
un·cha·ot·ic, *adjective* un·cha·ot·i·cal·ly, *adverb*
Antonyms
orderly, systematic.

chan·de·lier

noun
a decorative, sometimes ornate, light fixture suspended from a ceiling, usually having branched supports for a number of lights.

cir·cum·spect

adjective
1. watchful and discreet; cautious; prudent: **circumspect** behavior.
2. well-considered: **circumspect** ambition.

Origin:
1375–1425; late Middle English < Latin *circumspectus* (past participle of *circumspicere* to look around), equivalent to *circum-* circum- + *spec* (*ere*) to look + *-tus* past participle suffix

Related forms
cir·cum·spect·ly, *adverb*
cir·cum·spect·ness, *noun*
non·cir·cum·spect, *adjective*
non·cir·cum·spect·ly, *adverb*
non·cir·cum·spect·ness, *noun*
o·ver·cir·cum·spect, *adjective*
un·cir·cum·spect, *adjective*
un·cir·cum·spect·ly, *adverb*
un·cir·cum·spect·ness, *noun*

Synonyms
1. careful, vigilant, guarded.

Antonyms
1. careless, indiscreet.

clum·sy

adjective, clum·si·er, clum·si·est.
1. awkward in movement or action; without skill or grace: *He is very* **clumsy** *and is always breaking things.*
2. awkwardly done or made; unwieldy; ill-contrived: *He made a* **clumsy***, embarrassed apology.*

Origin:
1590–1600; *clums* benumbed with cold (now obsolete) + -y[1]; akin to Middle English *clumsen* to be stiff with cold, dialectal Swedish *klumsig* benumbed, awkward, *klums* numbskull, Old Norse *klumsa* lockjaw. See clam[2]

Related forms
clum·si·ly, *adverb*
clum·si·ness, *noun*

Synonyms
1. ungraceful, ungainly, lumbering, lubberly. **2.** unhandy, unskillful, maladroit, inexpert, bungling, bumbling, heavy-handed, inept.

Antonyms
2. adroit, skillful.

clut·ter

verb (used with object)
1. to fill or litter with things in a disorderly manner: *All kinds of papers* **clutter**ed *the top of his desk.*
verb (used without object)
2. *British Dialect* . to run in disorder; move with bustle and confusion.
3. *British Dialect* . to make a clatter.
4. to speak so rapidly and inexactly that distortions of sound and phrasing result.

noun
5. a disorderly heap or assemblage; litter: *It's impossible to find anything in all this* **clutter**.
6. a state or condition of confusion.
7. confused noise; clatter.
8. an echo or echoes on a radar screen that do not come from the target and can be caused by such factors as atmospheric conditions, objects other than the target, chaff, and jamming of the radar signal.

Origin:
1550–60; variant of *clotter* (now obsolete), equivalent to clot + -er⁶

Related forms
o·ver·clut·ter, *verb (used with object)*
un·clut·ter, *verb (used with object)*
un·clut·tered, *adjective*

Synonyms
5. mess, disorder, jumble.

con·fi·dence

noun
1. full trust; belief in the powers, trustworthiness, or reliability of a person or thing: *We have every* **confidence** *in their ability to succeed.*
2. belief in oneself and one's powers or abilities; self-**confidence**; self-reliance; assurance: *His lack of* **confidence** *defeated him.*
3. certitude; assurance: *He described the situation with such* **confidence** *that the audience believed him completely.*
4. a confidential communication: *to exchange* **confidence***s.*
5. (especially in European politics) the wish to retain an incumbent government in office, as shown by a vote in a particular issue: *a vote of* **confidence***.*
Origin:
1350–1400; Middle English (< Middle French) < Latin *confidentia.* See confide, -ence

Related forms
hy·per·con·fi·dence, *noun*
non·con·fi·dence, *noun*
su·per·con·fi·dence, *noun*

Synonyms
1. faith, reliance, dependence. See trust. **2.** CONFIDENCE, ASSURANCE both imply a faith in

oneself. **CONFIDENCE** may imply trust in oneself or arrogant self-conceit. ASSURANCE implies even more sureness of oneself; this may be shown as undisturbed **calm** or as offensive boastfulness.

Antonyms
1. mistrust.

con·sid·er·a·tion

noun
1. the act of considering; careful thought; meditation; deliberation: *I will give your project full* **consideration**.
2. something that is or is to be kept in mind in making a decision, evaluating facts, etc.: *Age was an important* **consideration** *in the decision.*
3. thoughtful or sympathetic regard or respect; thoughtfulness for others: *They showed no* **consideration** *for his feelings.*
4. a thought or reflection; an opinion based upon reflection.
5. a recompense or payment, as for work done; compensation.

des·per·ate

adjective
1. reckless or dangerous because of <u>despair</u> or urgency: *a **desperate** killer.*
2. having an urgent need, desire, etc.: ***desperate** for attention.*
3. leaving little or no hope; very serious or dangerous: *a **desperate** illness.*
4. extremely bad; intolerable or shocking: *clothes in **desperate** taste.*
5. extreme or excessive.

dis·heart·en

verb (used with object)
to depress the hope, courage, or spirits of; discourage.

dis·or·gan·ized

adjective
1. functioning without adequate order, systemization, or planning; uncoordinated: *a woefully **disorganized** enterprise.*
2. careless or undisciplined; sloppy: *too **disorganized** a person to be an agreeable roommate.*

Origin:
1805–15; disorganize + -ed²

Related forms
un·dis·or·gan·ized, *adjective*

Can be confused: disorganized, unorganized.

Synonyms
muddled, confused, disorderly, unsystematic.

dis·re·spect

transitive verb \ˌdis-ri-ˈspekt\
1: to have **disrespect** for
2: to show or express **disrespect** or contempt for :
INSULT, DIS <*disrespect*ed the officer> disrespectful

dis·tract·ed

adjective
1. having the attention diverted: *She tossed several rocks to the far left and slipped past the* **distracted** *sentry.*
2. rendered incapable of behaving, reacting, etc., in a normal manner, as by worry, remorse, or the like; irrational; disturbed.

e·lab·o·rate

adjective
1. worked out with great care and nicety of detail; executed with great minuteness: *elaborate preparations; elaborate* care. **Synonyms:** perfected, painstaking. **Antonyms:** simple.
2. marked by intricate and often excessive detail; complicated; ornate.
verb (used with object)
3. to work out carefully or minutely; develop to perfection. **Synonyms:** refine, improve.
4. to add details to; expand.
5. to produce or develop by labor.
6. *Physiology* . to convert (food, plasma, etc.) by means of chemical processes into a substance more suitable for use within the body.

[1]ex·as·per·ate

transitive verb \ig-ˈzas-pə-ˌrāt\
ex·as·per·at·edex·as·per·at·ing
1*a* : to excite the anger of : enrage
b : to cause irritation or annoyance to
2*obsolete* : to make more grievous : aggravate
calm(Antonym)

frenetically / fre·net·ic

adjective
frantic; frenzied.
Also, **fre·net·i·cal, phrenetic, phrenetical.**

Origin:
1350–1400; Middle English; see frantic

Related forms
fre·net·i·cal·ly, *adverb*
non·fre·net·ic, *adjective*
non·fre·net·i·cal·ly, *adverb*

frus·trat·ed

adjective
1. disappointed; thwarted: *an announcer who was a frustrated actor.*
2. having a feeling of or filled with frustration; dissatisfied: *His unresolved difficulty left him absolutely frustrated.*

fum·ble

verb (used without object)

1. to feel or grope about clumsily: *She **fumble**d in her purse for the keys.*
2. *Sports.* to **fumble** the ball.

verb (used with object)

3. to make, handle, etc., clumsily or inefficiently: *to **fumble** an attempt; He **fumble**d his way through the crowded room.*
4. *Sports.* to fail to hold or maintain hold on (a ball) after having touched it or carried it.

noun

5. the act of fumbling: *We completed the difficult experiment without a **fumble**.*
6. *Sports.* an act or instance of fumbling the ball.

Origin:
1500–10; akin to Norwegian, Swedish *fumla*, Middle Low German *fummeln* to grope, **fumble**

Related forms
fum·bler, *noun*
fum·bling·ly, *adverb*
fum·bling·ness, *noun*
out·fum·ble, *verb (used with object),* **out·fum·bled, out·fum·bling.**
un·fum·bled, *adjective*
un·fum·bling, *adjective*

Synonyms
3. bungle, botch, mishandle, spoil, muff.

¹glis·ten
intransitive verb \\'gli-sᵊn\\
: to give off a sparkling or lustrous reflection of or as if of a moist or polished surface

²glisten
noun
: GLITTER, SPARKLE

glum

adjective, glum·mer, glum·mest.
sullenly or silently gloomy; dejected.

Origin:
1425–75; late Middle English; variant of gloom

Related forms
glum·ly, *adverb*
glum·ness, *noun*

Synonyms
moody, sulky; despondent, melancholy. G‍LUM, MOROSE, SULLEN, DOUR, SURLY all are adjectives describing a gloomy, unsociable attitude. G‍LUM describes a depressed, spiritless condition or manner, usually temporary rather than habitual: *a glum shrug of the shoulders; a glum, hopeless look in his eye.* MOROSE which adds to GLUM a sense of bitterness, implies a habitual and pervasive gloominess: *a sour, morose manner; morose withdrawal from human contact.* SULLEN usually implies

reluctance or refusal to speak accompanied by glowering looks expressing anger or a sense of injury: *a sullen manner, silence, look.* DOUR refers to a stern and forbidding aspect, stony and unresponsive: *dour rejection of friendly overtures.* SURLY implies gruffness of speech and manner, usually accompanied by an air of injury and ill temper: *a surly reply.*

gran·di·ose
adjective \ˈgran-dē-ˌōs, ˌgran-dē-ˈ\
1: characterized by affectation of grandeur or splendor or by absurd exaggeration
2: impressive because of uncommon largeness, scope, effect, or grandeur
— **gran·di·ose·ly** *adverb*
— **gran·di·ose·ness** *noun*
— **gran·di·os·i·ty** \ˌgran -dē-ˈä -sə-tē\ *noun*

harsh
adjective \ˈhärsh \ 1
: having a coarse uneven surface that is rough or unpleasant to the touch
2*a* : causing a disagreeable or painful sensory reaction : IRRITATING
b : physically discomforting : PAINFUL
3: unduly exacting : SEVERE
4: lacking in aesthetic appeal or refinement : CRUDE
— **harsh·ly** *adverb*
— **harsh·ness** *noun*

haugh·ty

***adjective,* haugh·ti·er, haugh·ti·est.**
1. disdainfully proud; snobbish; scornfully arrogant; supercilious: **haughty** *aristocrats; a* **haughty** *salesclerk.*
2. *Archaic.* lofty or noble; exalted.

Origin:
1520–30; obsolete *haught* (spelling variant of late Middle English *haute* < Middle French < Latin *altus* high, with *h-* < Germanic; compare Old High German *hok* high) + -y¹

Related forms
haugh·ti·ly, *adverb*
haugh·ti·ness, *noun*
o·ver·haugh·ti·ly, *adverb*
o·ver·haugh·ti·ness, *noun*
o·ver·haugh·ty, *adjective*

Synonyms
1. lordly, disdainful, contemptuous. See proud.

Antonyms
1. humble, unpretentious, unassuming.

heed

verb (used with object)
1. to give careful attention to: *He did not* **heed** *the warning.*
verb (used without object)
2. to give attention; have regard.
noun
3. careful attention; notice; observation (usually with *give* or *take*).

in·de·cent

adjective
1. offending against generally accepted standards of propriety or good taste; improper; vulgar: **indecent** *jokes;* **indecent** language; **indecent** *behavior.*
2. not decent; unbecoming or unseemly: **indecent** *haste.*

Origin:
1555–65; < Latin *indecent-* (stem of *indecēns*) unseemly. See in-[3], decent

Related forms
in·de·cent·ly, *adverb*

Synonyms
1. distasteful, immodest, indecorous, indelicate; coarse, outrageous, rude, gross; obscene, filthy, lewd, licentious. See improper. **2.** inappropriate.

Antonyms
2. appropriate; becoming.

in·quis·i·tive

adjective
1. given to inquiry, research, or asking questions; eager for knowledge; intellectually curious: *an **inquisitive** mind.*
2. unduly or inappropriately curious; prying.
noun
3. an **inquisitive** person: *thick curtains to frustrate inquisitives.*

in·scribe

verb (used with object), **in·scribed, in·scrib·ing.**
1. to address or dedicate (a book, photograph, etc.) informally to a person, especially by writing a brief personal note in or on it.
2. to mark (a surface) with words, characters, etc., especially in a durable or conspicuous way.
3. to write, print, mark, or engrave (words, characters, etc.).
4. to enroll, as on an official list.
5. *Geometry*. to draw or delineate (one figure) within another figure so that the inner lies entirely within the boundary of the outer, touching it at as

many points as possible: *to **inscribe** a circle in a square.*

judg·ment

noun
1. an act or instance of judging.
2. the ability to judge, make a <u>decision</u>, or form an opinion objectively, authoritatively, and wisely, especially in matters affecting action; good sense; discretion: *a man of <u>sound</u> **judgment**.*
3. the demonstration or exercise of such ability or capacity: *The major was decorated for the **judgment** he showed under fire.*
4. the forming of an opinion, estimate, notion, or conclusion, as from circumstances presented to the mind: *Our **judgment** as to the cause of his failure must rest on the evidence.*
5. the opinion formed: *He regretted his hasty **judgment**.*

kind·ness

noun \ˈkĭn(d)-nəs\ **Kindness** \kĭn(d)-nəs\ Adjective
chrestos(greek): "serviceable, good, pleasant", gracious, kind.
  chrestotes(greek): Goodness of heart, gentleness.
    philanthropos(greek): humanely, kindly, courteously.
1 a kind deed : FAVOR

2a : the quality or state of being kind   **b** *archaic* : AFFECTION

See   Page 5.

lev·er

noun
1. *Mechanics* . a <u>rigid</u> bar that pivots about one point and that is used to move an <u>object</u> at a second point by a <u>force</u> applied at a third. Compare <u>machine</u> def 4b .
2. a means or agency of persuading or of achieving an end: *Saying that the chairman of the board likes the plan is just a* **lever** *to get us to support it.*
3. *Horology* . the pallet of an escapement.
verb* (used with object), <u>*verb*</u> *(used without object)
4. to move with or apply a **lever**: *to* **lever** *a rock; to* **lever** *mightily and to no avail*

¹men·ace

noun \' me-nəs\ / 1: a show of intention to inflict harm :

THREAT 2a : one that represents a threat : DANGER b : an annoying person .

mo·men·tar·i·ly

adverb
1. for a moment; briefly: *to pause **momentarily**.*
2. at any moment; imminently: *expected to occur **momentarily**.*
3. instantly.

Origin:
1645–55; momentary + -ly

Can be confused: currently, immediately, **momentarily,** now, presently, soon (see synonym study at immediately)(see usage note at presently).

ob·tru·sive

adjective
1. having or showing a disposition to obtrude, as by imposing oneself or one's opinions on others.
2. (of a thing) obtruding itself: *an **obtrusive** error.*
3. protruding; projecting.

po·lite

adjective, po·lit·er, po·lit·est.
1. showing good manners toward others, as in behavior, speech, etc.; courteous; civil: *a* **polite** *reply.*
2. refined or cultured: **polite** *society.*
3. of a refined or elegant kind: **polite** *learning.*

Origin:
1400–50; late Middle English < Latin *polītus*, past participle of *polīre* to polish

Related forms
po·lite·ly, *adverb*
po·lite·ness, *noun*
su·per·po·lite, *adjective*
su·per·po·lite·ly, *adverb*
su·per·po·lite·ness, *noun*

Synonyms
1. well-bred, gracious. See civil. **2.** urbane, polished, poised, courtly, cultivated.

Antonyms
1, 2. rude.

pro·duc·tive

adjective
1. having the power of producing; generative; creative: *a **productive** effort.*
2. producing readily or abundantly; fertile: *a **productive** vineyard.*
3. causing; bringing about (usually followed by *of*): *conditions **productive** of crime and sin.*
4. *Economics* , producing or tending to produce goods and services having exchange value.
5. *Grammar* . (of derivational affixes or patterns) readily used in forming new words, as the suffix *-ness.*

raspy

adjective \ˈras -pē\ 1: **HARSH**, GRATING 2: IRRITABLE

re·flect

verb (used with object)
1. to cast back (light, heat, sound, etc.) from a surface: *The mirror reflected the light onto the wall.*
2. to give back or show an image of; mirror.
3. (of an act or its result) to serve to cast or bring (credit, discredit, etc.) on its performer.
4. to reproduce; show: *followers reflecting the views of the leader.*
5. to throw or cast back; cause to return or rebound: *Her bitterness reflects gloom on all her family.*

re·fresh

verb (used with object)
1. to provide new vigor and energy by rest, food, etc. (often used reflexively).
2. to stimulate (the memory).
3. to make fresh again; reinvigorate or cheer (a person, the mind, spirits, etc.).
4. to freshen in appearance, color, etc., as by a restorative.
5. *Computers.* a. to display (an image) repeatedly, as on a CRT, in order to prevent fading.
b. to read and write (the contents of dynamic storage) at intervals in order to avoid loss of data.

re·group

verb (used with object)
1. to form into a new or restructured group or grouping.
verb (used without object)
2. to become reorganized in order to make a fresh start: *If the plan doesn't work, we'll have to regroup and try something else.*
3. *Military .* to become organized in a new tactical formation.

re·sound·ing

adjective
1. making an echoing sound: *a resounding thud.*

2. uttered loudly: *resounding speech.*
3. impressively thorough or complete: *a resounding popular success.*

re·spon·si·ble

adjective
1. answerable or accountable, as for something within one's power, control, or management (often followed by *to* or *for*): *He is responsible to the president for his decisions.*
2. involving accountability or responsibility: *a responsible position.*
3. chargeable with being the author, cause, or occasion of something (usually followed by *for*): *Termites were responsible for the damage.*
4. having a capacity for moral decisions and therefore accountable; capable of rational thought or action: *The defendant is not responsible for his actions.*
5. able to discharge obligations or pay debts.

reap

verb (used with object)
1. to cut (wheat, rye, etc.) with a sickle or other implement or a machine, as in harvest.
2. to gather or take (a crop, harvest, etc.).

3. to get as a return, recompense, or result: *to reap large profits.*
verb (used without object)
4. to reap a crop, harvest, etc.

Origin:
before 900; Middle English *repen,* Old English *repan, riopan;* cognate with Middle Low German *repen* to ripple (flax); akin to ripe

Related forms
reap·a·ble, *adjective*
un·reaped, *adjective*

Synonyms
3. gather, earn, realize, gain, win.

repentantly / re·pent·ant

adjective
1. repenting; penitent; experiencing repentance.
2. characterized by or showing repentance: *a repentant mood.*

Origin:
1250–1300; Middle English *repentaunt* < Old French *repentant* (present participle of *repentir*). See repent[1], -ant

Related forms

re·pent·ant·ly, *adverb*
half-re·pent·ant, *adjective*
non·re·pent·ant, *adjective*
non·re·pent·ant·ly, *adverb*
un·re·pent·ant, *adjective*

sarcastically / sar·casm

noun
1. harsh or bitter derision or irony.
2. a sharply ironical taunt; sneering or cutting remark: *a review full of sarcasms.*

Origin:
1570–80; < Late Latin *sarcasmus* < Greek *sarkasmós,* derivative of *sarkázein* to rend (flesh), sneer; see sarco-

Related forms
su·per·sar·casm, *noun*

Synonyms
1. sardonicism, bitterness, ridicule. See irony[1]. **2.** jeer.

scat·tered

adjective

1. distributed or occurring at widely spaced and usually irregular intervals: *scattered villages; scattered showers.*
2. dispersed; **disorganized**: *scattered forces.*
3. **distracted** or **disorganized**: *scattered thoughts.*
4. *Meteorology*. (of clouds) covering up to one-half of the sky. Compare broken def 5.

scur·ry / scurrying

verb (used without object)
1. to go or move quickly or in haste.
verb (used with object)
2. to send hurrying along.
noun
3. a scurrying rush: *the scurry of little feet on the stairs.*
4. a short run or race.

Origin:
1800–10; extracted from hurry-scurry

Shine (Shone)

1

verb (used without object)
1. to give forth or glow with light; shed or cast light.
2. to be bright with reflected light; **glisten**; sparkle.

3. (of light) to appear brightly or strongly, especially uncomfortably so: *Wear dark glasses so the sun won't* **shine** *in your eyes.*
4. to be or appear unusually animated or bright, as the eyes or face.
5. to appear with brightness or clearness, as feelings.
6. to excel or be conspicuous: *to* **shine** *in school.*
verb (used with object)
7. to cause to **shine**.
8. to direct the light of (a lamp, mirror, etc.): **Shine** *the flashlight on the steps so I can see.*
9. to put a gloss or polish on; polish (as shoes, silverware, etc.).
noun
10. radiance or brightness caused by emitted or reflected light.
11. luster; polish.
12. sun**shine**; fair weather.
13. a polish or gloss given to shoes.
14. an act or instance of polishing shoes.
15. *Informal.* a foolish prank; caper.
16. *Slang: Disparaging and Offensive.* a black person.
Verb phrases
17. **shine up to,** *Informal.*
a. to attempt to impress (a person), especially in order to gain benefits for oneself.
b. to become especially attentive to (one of the opposite sex): *Men* **shine** *up to her like moths to a light.*
Idioms
18. **come rain or shine,**
a. regardless of the weather.
b. no matter what the circumstances may be: *Come rain or* **shine**, *he is always on the job.*
Also, **rain or shine**.
19. **take a shine to,** *Informal.* to take a liking or fancy to: *That little girl has really taken a* **shine** *to you.*

smug

adjective, **smug·ger, smug·gest.**
1. contentedly confident of one's ability, superiority, or correctness; complacent.
2. trim; spruce; smooth; sleek.

sob

verb (used without object)
1. to weep with a convulsive catching of the breath.
2. to make a <u>sound</u> resembling this.
verb (used with object)
3. to utter with **sob**s.
4. to put, send, etc., by **sob**bing or with **sob**s: *to sob oneself to sleep.*
noun
5. the act of **sob**bing; a convulsive catching of the breath in weeping.
6. any sound suggesting this.

Origin:
1150–1200; Middle English *sobben,* apparently imitative

Related forms
sob·ber, *noun*
sob·bing·ly, *adverb*
sob·ful, *adjective*

sol·i·tar·y

adjective
1. alone; without companions; unattended: *a **solitary** passer-by*.
2. living alone; avoiding the society of others: *a **solitary** existence*.
3. by itself; alone: *one **solitary** house*.
4. characterized by the absence of companions: *a **solitary** journey*.
5. done without assistance or accompaniment; done in solitude: ***solitary** chores*.

SOW

[1]

verb (used with object)
1. to scatter (seed) over land, earth, etc., for growth; plant.
2. to plant seed for: *to **sow** a crop*.
3. to scatter seed over (land, earth, etc.) for the purpose of growth.
4. to implant, introduce, or promulgate; seek to propagate or extend; disseminate: *to **sow** distrust or dissension*.
5. to strew or sprinkle with anything.

verb (used without object)
6. to **sow** seed, as for the production of a crop.

state·ly
adjective \-lē\
1
a : marked by lofty or imposing dignity
b : **HAUGHTY**, UNAPPROACHABLE
2
: impressive in size or proportions

¹stern•ly
adjective \ˈstəm\ 1a : having a definite hardness or severity of nature or manner : AUSTERE *b* : expressive of severe displeasure : HARSH 2: forbidding or gloomy in appearance 3: INEXORABLE <*stern* necessity> 4: STURDY, STOUT <a *stern* resolve> — **stern·ly** *adverb*

sternly / stern

¹

adjective, stern·er, stern·est.
1. firm, **strict**, or uncompromising: *stern discipline.*
2. hard, **harsh**, or severe: *a stern reprimand.*
3. rigorous or austere; of an unpleasantly serious character: *stern times.*
4. grim or forbidding in aspect: *a stern face.*

Origin:
before 1000; Middle English; Old English *styrne*

Related forms
stern·ly, *adverb*
stern·ness, *noun*

Synonyms
1, 2. adamant, unrelenting, unsympathetic, cruel, unfeeling. STERN, SEVERE, **HARSH** agree in referring to methods, aspects, manners, or facial expressions. STERN implies uncompromising, inflexible firmness, and sometimes a hard, forbidding, or withdrawn aspect or nature: *a stern parent.* SEVERE implies **strict**ness, lack of sympathy, and a tendency to impose a hard discipline on others: *a severe judge.* **HARSH** suggests a great severity and roughness, and cruel, unfeeling treatment of others: *a **harsh** critic.*

Antonyms
1. lenient.

strict

adjective \ˈstrikt\ 1
archaic
a : TIGHT, CLOSE; *also* : INTIMATE

b : NARROW

2a : stringent in requirement or control <under **strict** orders>
b : severe in discipline <a **strict** teacher>
3a : inflexibly maintained or adhered to <**strict** secrecy>
b : rigorously conforming to principle or a norm or condition
4: EXACT, PRECISE <in the **strict** sense of the word>
5: of narrow erect habit of growth <a **strict** inflorescence>
— **strict·ly** \ˈstrik(t)-lē\ *adverb*
— **strict·ness** \-nəs\ *noun*

stu·di·ous

adjective
1. disposed or given to diligent study: *a **studious** boy.*
2. concerned with, characterized by, or pertaining to study: ***studious** tastes.*
3. zealous, assiduous, or painstaking: ***studious** care.*
4. carefully planned or maintained; studied: *a **studious** program to maintain peace.*
5. devoted to or favorable for study

swift

adjective
1. moving or capable of moving with great speed or velocity; fleet; rapid: *a **swift** ship.*
2. coming, happening, or performed quickly or without delay: *a **swift** decision.*
3. quick or prompt to act or respond: ***swift** to jump to conclusions.*
4. *Slang.* quick to perceive or understand; smart; clever: *You can't cheat him, he's too **swift**.*
adverb
5. **swift**ly.

ten·der

1

adjective
1. soft or delicate in substance; not hard or tough: *a **tender** steak.*
2. weak or delicate in constitution; not strong or hardy.
3. (of plants) unable to withstand freezing temperatures.
4. young or immature: *children of **tender** age.*
5. delicate or soft in quality: ***tender** blue.*

ter·ror:

noun \'ter-ər, 'te-rər\ **1:** a state of intense fear **2a :** one that inspires fear : SCOURGE **b :** a frightening aspect <the ***terrors*** of invasion>

tran·quil

adjective \'traŋ-kwəl,¹ tran

a : free from agitation of mind or spirit <a ***tranquil*** self-assurance>
b : free from disturbance or turmoil <a ***tranquil*** scene>
2
: unvarying in aspect : STEADY, STABLE

— **tran·quil·ly** \-kwə-lē\ *adverb*
— **tran·quil·ness** *noun*

vir·tue

noun \ˈvər-(\)tchü\ conformity to a standard of right : MORALITY   *b* : a particular moral excellence   3: a beneficial quality or power of a thing   4: manly strength or courage : VALOR
5: a commendable quality or trait : MERIT   6: a capacity to act : POTENCY

1

Kindness Key of Conduct Prayer

Dear Heavenly Father,

I vow to be kind to everyone and to treat everyone with grace, respect, **kindness**, and love. This is the way I would like to be treated. I promise to do unto others as I would have them to do unto me. Thank you for teaching and helping me to be kind to everyone.

In Jesus name I pray.

Amen.

PRAYER FOR SALVATION

AND BAPTISM IN THE HOLY SPIRIT

Heavenly Father, I come to You today in the name of Jesus. Father forgive me of my sins. I ask Jesus to come into my heart and be Lord over my life (Romans 10:9-10, Romans 5:10, and Acts 2:21). I confess that Jesus is Lord and I believe in my heart that God raised Him from the dead (1 Cor. 15:20-25).

Thank you Lord Jesus! Now I am reborn! I am a Christian - a very victorious child of Almighty God! I am saved!

Father I'm also asking You to fill me with the Holy Spirit. Holy Spirit I receive you and I welcome you into my heart. I fully expect to speak with other tongues as You give me the utterance (Acts 1:8; Acts 2:4; 1Cor. 14:2; Luke

11:13).

Hallelujah! Thank You Jesus!

About the Author

Ms. Misha Grace Benjamin is the Founder and President of The Wordflowers Corporation. Wordflowers is a Christian Publishing Company that speaks and distinctively praises God's Word in the earth. At Wordflowers, Ms. Benjamin is also a Writer and Author who specializes in Christian and Children's Literature. Ms. Benjamin is a graduate of the Institute of Children's Literature. Ms. Benjamin also works as a Volunteer Teacher for English Speakers of Other Languages (ESOL) and also as a Children's Story-Time Reader. Ms. Benjamin currently resides in Woodbridge, VA.

Other Books Written by the Author

- **Inviting Jesus Into Your Heart:** *Understanding your new life as a born again Believer*

- **Agape's Performance**

- **Egypt, Assyria, Israel, and their God**

For More Information about Wordflowers

Your questions, inquiries, and requests for more information are welcome at:

info@wordflowerscorp.org

You may also visit our website at: www.wordflowers.org.

References & Sources

1. *dictionary.reference.com*

2. *merriam-webster.com*

3. *Vine's concise Dictionary of the Bible, Published in Nashville, Tennessee, by Thomas Nelson, Inc, 1999.*

www.ingramcontent.com/pod-product-compliance
Lightning Source LLC
Chambersburg PA
CBHW031239290426
44109CB00012B/356